LIQUOR

LOLLIPOPS

LIP-SMACKING HARD CANDY RECIPES

KRISTINA MAURY

Quarto Publishing Group USA Inc.
142 West 36th Street, 4th Floor
New York, NY 10018

ROCK POINT and the distinctive Rock Point Publishing logo
are trademarks of Quarto Publishing Group USA Inc.

ISBN: 978-1-63106-115-8

Library of Congress Cataloging-in-Publication data is
available

Photography: Rick Schwab
Photo Shoot Art Direction and Prop Styling: Heidi North
Interior Design: Heidi North

Printed in China

10 9 8 7 6 5 4 3 2 1

www.rockpointpub.com

CONTENTS

. . . .

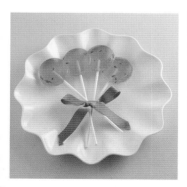

INTRODUCTION
TO HARD CANDY MAKING

The idea of making hard candy can be scary to those who have never done it. The thought of having to use a candy thermometer alone is enough to make some people shy away. In reality, hard candy making is very simple if you follow the directions. And, contrary to popular belief, you don't need fancy equipment.

One of my favorite things about hard candy is its versatility. It's amazing how you can turn a cup of sugar, a few tablespoons of corn syrup, and a bit of water into little pieces of culinary art that are just as beautiful as they are delicious. There is simply no end to the different combinations of flavors, colors, and ingredients you can use to create unique hard candies. I founded my company, Luxe Lollies, with this versatility in mind.

Candy and cocktails are two of my favorite things, so naturally cocktail-inspired lollipops were some of the first candies that I started selling. The liquor lollipop recipes in this book won't get you tipsy since most of the alcohol burns off during cooking, but the flavor of the liquor you used will remain. Think of these as cocktail-inspired lollipops rather than cocktails in lollipop form.

If you like to entertain like I do, knowing how to make gourmet lollipops is a skill that will come in handy. Handmade lollipops are not only a great addition to your personal candy stash, but they make perfect party favors and gifts. Have fun experimenting with different ways to display and package your lollipops!

The Basics

Read the Recipe Before Cooking

I cannot express enough how important it is to read each recipe through before starting to make a batch of candy. Sugar can burn very quickly so it is important to have everything prepared beforehand and to avoid distractions. You'll want to keep your eyes on the stove at all times.

The Importance of a Candy Thermometer

I've burned enough batches to know that a candy/deep-fry thermometer is a necessity when making hard candy. Cooked sugar goes through different stages as the temperature rises. To make hard candy, you must reach the hard-crack stage, which is at 300–310 degrees F. It's very important to remove the pot from the stove at 300 degrees because the mix rises in temperature rapidly. Leaving it on the stove just a few seconds longer will most likely result in a burnt, inedible, smelly mess. Don't be alarmed if your sugar yellows while cooking; that is perfectly normal. When sugar reaches the hard-crack stage it generally turns light golden in color. If it turns amber and smells burnt then you have

a problem. However, if you're using dark liquor, the mixture will take on that color.

Unfortunately, inexpensive candy thermometers are notoriously unreliable. While you can get a candy thermometer at your local grocery store, don't be surprised if it stops working after your first use (sometimes they don't even work the first time). It's best to invest in a quality thermometer from a cooking store like Williams-Sonoma.

Either way, you'll always want to test your thermometer before you begin. It may seem like a pain, but it's better than the alternative (a burnt batch of candy). To test your candy thermometer, place it in a bit of boiling water. If it is working correctly it will read 212 degrees F/100 degrees C (if you're at sea level). If you're at a higher altitude water will boil at a lower temperature. If you're lower than sea level, water will boil at a higher temperature.

If, during cooking, your thermometer stops working (or you suspect it has stopped working), you can do the cold-water test to determine when the candy has reached hard crack stage. Using a spoon, drop a small amount of the hot sugar mixture into a glass of very cold water. Allow the syrup to cool off a bit in the water before pulling it out. If it has formed into hard, brittle threads and breaks when it is bent, the mixture has reached hard-crack stage. This method isn't recommended as a replacement for a thermometer because it takes your attention away from the stove.

Safety

While you'll want to work quickly when the sugar mixture reaches the required temperature, you'll also want to work safely. Gloves are a must. Trust me, I've burned myself enough times to know hot sugar is no joke—I have the scars to prove it. I use heat-resistant silicone gloves, but rubber-cleaning gloves are fine for the casual confectioner.

Cookware

You can use any heavy pot as long as it is 1–2 quarts in capacity. If you use a larger pot, your candy will most likely burn. Copper is the best pot for candy making as it is a great heat conductor and ensures the candy cooks evenly, but it really isn't necessary. To clean hard candy that becomes stuck to your pot, simply soak the pot in hot water or fill the pot with water and boil it until the candy melts.

Molds

There are a wide variety of molds on the market in hundreds of shapes and sizes. It is very important that you use molds that are made for hard candy. If you use a mold made specifically for chocolate, it will melt since it can't handle the heat of hard candy. Most hard candy molds are opaque white in color while chocolate molds are clear. You can also use silicone candy molds, but they are more expensive.

There are 3 basic flat, round lollipop molds that I use in my business: $1\frac{1}{2}$-inch (38.1 mm) in diameter molds, 2-inch (50.8 mm) in diameter molds, and $2\frac{1}{2}$-inch (63.5 mm) in diameter molds. The recipe serving sizes in this book are based on the 2-inch (50.8 mm) in diameter molds. I wouldn't recommend the $1\frac{1}{2}$-inch (38.1 mm) mold for most of the recipes in this book because it's simply too small to showcase many of the decorative ingredients called for.

While you can make lollipops without molds, if you've never made hard candy before, I recommend starting with molds to get a hang of the pouring process. Lollipops made without molds have a more rustic, handmade look that some people prefer. You'll notice that the serving size for lollipops made with molds and lollipops made without molds is different. This is because lollipops made without molds are much thinner; thus, you can make more at once. I personally prefer the more substantial molded lollipop. If making lollipops without molds, you'll need a silicone baking mat, a baking sheet, and a steady hand. Most of the recipes in this book give directions using both methods. Some recipes are better suited to one method than the other and will only include the preferred method. As noted in the recipes, if you're making lollipops without molds, the candy mixture needs to harden a bit before pouring, otherwise you'll have messy lollipops with no recognizable shape.

You can find lollipop molds at your local craft and baking/candy-supply stores. I order my molds online because I find that the prices are better and there is more variety. I recommend the following online suppliers: getsuckered.com, candylandcrafts.com, confectioneryhouse.com, lorannoils.com, and countrykitchensa.com. You can also find molds on eBay and Amazon.

Lollipop Sticks

Lollipop sticks can also be found at your local craft and baking/candy-supply store or at any of the websites mentioned above. They come in various lengths.

Pastry Brush

Every recipe in this book calls for a pastry brush to wash sugar crystals down the side of the pot while cooking (if needed). This will help to ensure that dry sugar granules aren't introduced into the batch during the cooking process since that could cause crystallization (grainy candy). I find that I usually don't have to do this, but I keep a pastry brush on hand just in case. If you don't have a brush, you can put a lid on the pot for about a minute at the beginning of cooking. This will cause the steam to wash away any dry sugar crystals that are on the sides of the pot.

Shelf Life and Storage

Sugar is a natural preservative so technically most hard candies won't go bad. Moisture is the enemy of hard candy. When storing your candy you'll want to keep this in mind. Some of the recipes in this book call for fresh ingredients like fruit slices and herbs. These ingredients introduce moisture into the candy and make the shelf life shorter. If using fresh fruit and herbs, you'll want to consume them within a couple of days. Otherwise, for short-term storage, airtight containers or Ziploc® bags are fine. (If you live in a humid environment, silica gel packets would further ensure that the candy doesn't get sticky). If you plan on keeping the lollipops in storage for several weeks or more, foil zipper bags with silica gel packets are the way to go.

INGREDIENT NOTES

Alcohol

Using liquor is a quick and convenient way to flavor hard candy. Though most of the recipes in this book call for candy oil flavoring as well as liquor, you can get creative and develop your own candy flavors by using liquor alone. Making lollipops with liquor is a fun way to utilize infused alcohol and the ever-growing selection of flavored alcohols in the market. Most of the alcohol does burn off during the cooking process so the result will be a subtly flavored, cocktail-inspired lollipop rather than a cocktail in lollipop form. In other words, you can have as many as you want without worrying about who's going to be the designated driver!

All of the recipes in this book call for hard alcohol (whiskey, rum, tequila, vodka, and gin). You'll want to use alcohol that is at least 60-proof (30% alcohol by volume), but higher is preferable. The higher proof alcohol you use, the more the alcohol flavor will come through. Some of the recipes call for flavored liquor, which generally has a lower proof (there are exceptions—for instance, Captain Morgan makes both a 90-proof and a 42-proof coconut-flavored rum). Don't feel the need to splurge on fancy liquor—any subtle distinctions between particular brands of liquor will be drowned out by the sugar.

An additional note on liquor: bourbon tends to bubble a lot when cooking, so use slightly lower heat than you would use for other liquors.

Flavoring

When making hard candy, you'll want to use candy oil flavorings or essential oils rather than extracts. Candy oils and essential oils are much more concentrated than extracts. Since hard candy gets so hot, oil-based flavorings are better than alcohol-based extracts because more of the flavor is retained during cooking. You'd have to use a lot of extract to get decent flavoring whereas with candy oils and essential oils, a little goes a long way. There are three candy-oil suppliers that I purchase from: getsuckered.com, lorannoils.com and shop.perfumersapprentice.com. LorAnn Oils are also available at craft stores and cooking/baking-supply shops. Getsuckered.com has the largest variety of flavors. Different brands can vary in taste and in strength, but generally you should use about $1/4$ teaspoon per cup of sugar. With essential oils, you'll generally only use a drop. If you're using a natural candy oil, you'll usually need to use more (with the exception of strong flavors like peppermint which you'll only need a few drops of). If I prefer to use a particular brand in a recipe, I have made note of it in the ingredients list. On a related note, I've found that the flavors develop more when the lollipops are eaten the day after they are made.

Food Coloring

I use liquid or gel food coloring in my recipes. Liquid food coloring can easily be found at grocery stores, but gel food coloring comes in so many more colors. In addition, gel food coloring lasts longer—a little goes a long way. To create opaque lollipops, I use Wilton's White Icing Color, which can be purchased at craft and baking stores.

TROUBLESHOOTING

1. Your lollipops are sticky or won't harden: possible causes are high humidity and/ or rain or a broken thermometer. Hard candy can be finicky so you'll want to avoid making it on rainy or humid days. If it's always humid or rainy where you are, use a dehumidifier or turn on your air conditioner. If moisture in the air isn't an issue, then you probably are dealing with a broken thermometer that caused you to take the candy off of the stove too soon. In my experience, broken thermometers usually result in burned rather than undercooked candy.

2. Your candy burnt before reaching 300 degrees: this is most likely the result of a thermometer that is not accurately reading the temperature.

3. Your candy has a grainy or rough texture: this is caused by humidity and/or rain or by the introduction of dry sugar crystals during the cooking process. See first troubleshooting issue for methods on how to deal with moisture in the air. If high humidity isn't your issue, then make sure you are wiping down the sides of your pan with a pastry brush to remove sugar crystals are sticking on the sides of the pan.

BASIC LIQUOR LOLLIPOP RECIPE

Makes 8–15 lollipops • Prep Time: 10 minutes • Cook Time: 15 minutes • Cooling Time: 15 minutes

Vegetable oil cooking spray (if using molds)

Lollipop sticks

¼ cup (60mL) + 1 tablespoon (15mL) hard alcohol (rum, whiskey, vodka, tequila, or gin), divided

2 tablespoons (30mL) water

¾ cup (150g) granulated sugar

3 tablespoons (245g) light corn syrup

¼ teaspoon (1.25mL) candy oil flavoring (optional)

Food coloring (optional)

Lollipop bags

Twist ties

If using molds:

1a. Lightly coat lollipop molds with cooking spray. Position the lollipop sticks in the grooves of the molds.

If not using molds:

1b. Place a silicone mat on a baking sheet. Position the lollipop sticks on the mat about 3 inches (76.2mm) apart so there is enough room between each lollipop.

2. Combine ¼ cup (60 mL) hard alcohol, water, sugar, and corn syrup in a 1- or 2-quart saucepan. Place pan over medium heat to dissolve sugar. Use a wet pastry brush to "wash down" any sugar crystals that form on the side of the pan. Continue to cook the mixture without stirring until a candy thermometer registers 300 degrees.

3. Remove the pan from heat and carefully stir in food coloring (optional), candy oil flavoring (optional), and remaining tablespoon (15mL) hard alcohol.

If using molds:

4a. Slowly pour mixture into prepared lollipop molds.

If not using molds:

4b. Let the mixture cool for about 2 minutes then slowly pour over the sticks on the silicone mat. Adjust the lollipop sticks as needed, being careful not to touch the hot candy (the sticks should be inserted about halfway into the lollipop).

5. Let cool completely until lollipops harden and are no longer hot (about 15 minutes). Remove the lollipops from the molds or the silicone mat and wrap in lollipop bags with twist ties.

LIQUOR
LOLLIPOP

RECIPES

SPICED RUM CIDER

This seasonally inspired recipe is especially festive if you use thin cinnamon sticks in place of lollipop sticks. By using cinnamon sticks, plastic sticks, or wooden sticks the lollipops can double as drink stirrers. Stir the lollipop into warm rum to impart the taste of cinnamon, apples, and clove. These make a unique fall hostess gifts or party favors.

Makes 8–15 lollipops • Prep Time: 15 minutes • Cook Time: 15 minutes • Cooling Time: 15 minutes

1 bag cinnamon apple spice tea

¼ cup (60mL) + 1 tablespoon (15 mL) dark rum, divided

Vegetable oil cooking spray (if using molds)

Lollipop sticks

Small handful whole cloves

2 tablespoons (30mL) water

¾ cup (150g) granulated sugar

3 tablespoons (245g) light corn syrup

Lollipop bags

Twist ties

Note: While whole cloves are edible, they are strong tasting, making them very undesirable to eat whole. Please discard them as you eating the candy.

1. In a small bowl, steep tea bag in ¼ cup (60mL) rum for 5 minutes. Discard the tea bag.

If using molds:
2. Lightly coat lollipop molds with cooking spray and place a few cloves in the cavities of each mold. Position the lollipop sticks in the grooves of the molds.

If not using molds:
2a. Place a silicone mat on a baking sheet. Position the lollipop sticks on the mat about 3 inches (76.2mm) apart so there is enough room between each lollipop. Place a few cloves above each stick where you intend to pour the candy syrup.

3. Combine ¼ cup (60mL) tea-infused rum, water, sugar, and corn syrup in a 1- or 2-quart saucepan. Place pan over medium heat to dissolve sugar. Use a wet pastry brush to "wash down" any sugar crystals that form on the side of the pan. Continue to cook the mixture without stirring until a candy thermometer registers 300 degrees.

4. Remove pan from the heat and carefully stir in remaining tablespoon (15mL) rum.

If using molds:
5a. Slowly pour mixture into prepared lollipop molds.

If not using molds:
5b. Let the mixture cool for about 2 minutes then, using a spoon, slowly pour over the cloves. Adjust the lollipop sticks as needed, being careful not to touch the hot candy (the sticks should be inserted about halfway into the lollipop).

6. Let cool completely until lollipops harden and are no longer hot (about 15 minutes). Remove the lollipops from the molds or the silicone mat and wrap in lollipop bags with twist ties.

MOJITO

For a twist on the classic mojito, you can add fruit flavored candy oil or use flavored rum in this recipe. Pineapple is an especially tasty flavor addition.

Makes 8–15 lollipops • Prep Time: 10 minutes • Cook Time: 15 minutes • Cooling Time: 15 minutes

Vegetable oil cooking spray (if using molds)

Lollipop sticks

1 bunch fresh mint leaves

¼ cup (60mL) + 1 tablespoon (15 mL) white rum, divided

2 tablespoons (30 mL) water

¾ cup (50g) granulated sugar

½ teaspoon (2.5mL) natural lime oil

3 tablespoons (245g) light corn syrup

A drop neon green food coloring (or a drop green and a drop yellow food coloring, optional)

Lollipop bags

Twist ties

If using molds:
1a. Lightly coat lollipop molds with cooking spray and place 1–2 mint leaves in the cavities of each mold. Position the lollipop sticks in the grooves of the molds.

If not using molds:
1b. Place a silicone mat on a baking sheet. Position the lollipop sticks on the mat about 3 inches (76.2mm) apart so there is enough room between each lollipop. Place 1–2 mint leaves above each stick where you intend to pour the candy syrup.

2. Combine ¼ cup (60mL) rum, water, sugar, natural lime oil, and corn syrup in a 1- or 2-quart saucepan. Place pan over medium heat to dissolve sugar. Use a wet pastry brush to "wash down" any sugar crystals that form on the side of the pan. Continue to cook the mixture without stirring until a candy thermometer registers 300 degrees.

3. Remove the pan from heat and carefully stir in food coloring (optional) and remaining tablespoon (15mL) rum.

If using molds:
4a. Slowly pour mixture into prepared lollipop molds.

If not using molds:
4b. Let the mixture cool for about 2 minutes then, using a spoon, slowly pour over the mint leaves. Adjust the lollipop sticks as needed, being careful not to touch the hot candy (the sticks should be inserted about halfway into the lollipop).

5. Let cool completely until lollipops harden and are no longer hot (about 15 minutes). Remove the lollipops from the molds or the silicone mat and wrap in lollipop bags with twist ties.

CARIBBEAN RUM PUNCH

Two colors create a pretty watercolor effect reminiscent of a tropical sunset. For a fun party favor display, insert a block of floral foam or Styrofoam into a low glass vase. Pour sand in the vase, covering up the foam completely. Insert the lollipops into the foam, and add a few cocktail umbrellas for an extra-special touch.

Makes 8–15 lollipops • Prep Time: 15 minutes • Cook Time: 15 minutes • Cooling Time: 15 minutes

Vegetable oil cooking spray (if using molds)

Lollipop sticks

½ teaspoon (.9g) orange zest

¼ cup (60mL)+ 1 tablespoon (15 mL) white rum, divided

2 tablespoons (30mL) water

¾ cup (150g) granulated sugar

3 tablespoons (245g) light corn syrup

⅛ teaspoon pomegranate candy oil

⅛ teaspoon pineapple candy oil

⅛ teaspoon orange candy oil

⅛ teaspoon lime candy oil

1 drop yellow food coloring

1 drop orange food coloring

Pinch of nutmeg

Lollipop bags

Twist ties

If using molds:

1a. Lightly coat lollipop molds with cooking spray and place a bit of orange zest in the cavities of each mold. Position the lollipop sticks in the grooves of the molds.

If not using molds:

1b. Place a silicone mat on a baking sheet. Position the lollipop sticks on the mat about 3 inches (76.2mm) apart so there is enough room between each lollipop. Place a bit of orange zest above each stick where you intend to pour the candy syrup.

2. Combine ¼ cup (60mL) rum, water, sugar, and corn syrup in a 1- or 2-quart saucepan. Place pan over medium heat to dissolve sugar. Use a wet pastry brush to "wash down" any sugar crystals that form on the side of the pan. Continue to cook the mixture without stirring until a candy thermometer registers 300 degrees.

3. Remove the pot from heat and carefully stir in the remaining tablespoon (15mL) rum, candy oils, and nutmeg. To create a two-tone watercolor color effect, add a drop yellow food coloring and a drop orange food coloring spaced apart. Using a spoon, gently swirl the mix in a figure-eight pattern.

If using molds:

4a. Slowly pour mixture into prepared lollipop molds.

If not using molds:

4b. Let the mixture cool for about 2 minutes then, using a spoon, slowly pour over the orange zest. Adjust the lollipop sticks as needed, being careful not to touch the hot candy (the sticks should be inserted about halfway into the lollipop).

5. Let cool completely until lollipops harden and are no longer hot (about 15 minutes). Remove the lollipops from the molds or the silicone mat and wrap in lollipop bags with twist ties.

CHOCOLATE SNOWBALL

Chocolate and coconut lovers will adore these lollipops! Because this recipe calls for coconut flakes to be added after the candy is poured, it's best to make them without molds so the coconut will be on the front of the lollipops rather than the back.

Makes 15 lollipops • Prep Time: 10 minutes • Cook Time: 15 minutes • Cooling Time: 15 minutes

Lollipop sticks

¼ cup (60mL) + 1 tablespoon (15mL) coconut rum, divided

2 tablespoons (30mL) water

¾ cup (150g) granulated sugar

3 tablespoons (245g) light corn syrup

¼ teaspoon (1.25mL) LorAnn's chocolate hazelnut candy oil

2–3 drops white food coloring

2–3 drops brown food coloring

2 tablespoons (35g) dried coconut flakes

Powdered sugar

Lollipop bags

Twist ties

1. Place a silicone mat on a baking sheet. Position the lollipop sticks on the mat about 3 inches (76.2mm) apart so there is enough room between each lollipop.

2. Combine ¼ cup (60mL) rum, water, sugar, and corn syrup in a 1- or 2-quart saucepan. Place pan over medium heat to dissolve sugar. Use a wet pastry brush to "wash down" any sugar crystals that form on the side of the pan. Continue to cook the mixture without stirring until a candy thermometer registers 300 degrees.

3. Remove pan from heat and carefully stir in the remaining tablespoon (15mL) rum and candy oil.

4. Stir in white food coloring and then the brown food coloring. Stir until both colors are completely mixed and you have an opaque chocolate brown color, adding more brown food coloring a drop at a time if needed.

5. Let the mixture cool for about 2 minutes then, using a spoon, slowly pour onto the silicone mat over the lollipop sticks. Adjust the lollipop sticks as needed, being careful not to touch the hot candy (the sticks should be inserted about halfway into the lollipop). Sprinkle a generous amount of coconut flakes onto each lollipop. Top each lollipop off with a dusting of powdered sugar.

6. Let cool completely until lollipops harden and are no longer hot (about 15 minutes). Remove the lollipops from the silicone mat and wrap in lollipop bags with twist ties.

CHOCOLATE PEPPERMINT MARTINI

These festive lollipops not only make fun stocking stuffers and gift toppers, but they are great to stir into a glass of hot cocoa or coffee (use plastic lollipop sticks). If you use molds, the peppermint pieces will melt into the hot candy mixture and create a pretty stained glass effect.

Makes 8–15 lollipops • Prep Time: 15 minutes • Cook Time: 15 minutes • Cooling Time: 15 minutes

Vegetable oil cooking spray (if using molds)

Lollipop sticks

¼ cup (326g) crushed peppermint candy

¼ cup (60mL) + 1 tablespoon (15mL) peppermint bark vodka, divided

2 tablespoons (30mL) water

¾ cup (150g) granulated sugar

3 tablespoons (245g) light corn syrup

2–3 drops white food coloring

2–3 drops brown food coloring

Lollipop bags

Twist ties

If using molds:
1a. Lightly coat lollipop molds with cooking spray. Sprinkle a bit of the crushed peppermint candy in the cavities of each mold (no more than half-way). Position the lollipop sticks in the grooves of the molds.

If not using molds:
1b. Place a silicone mat on a baking sheet. Position the lollipop sticks on the mat about 3 inches (76.2mm) apart so there is enough room between each lollipop. (The peppermint pieces will be added at the end.)

2. Combine ¼ cup (60mL) vodka, water, sugar, and corn syrup in a 1- or 2-quart saucepan. Place pan over medium heat to dissolve sugar. Use a wet pastry brush to "wash down" any sugar crystals that form on the side of the pan. Continue to cook the mixture without stirring until a candy thermometer registers 300 degrees.

3. Remove the pan from heat and carefully stir in the remaining tablespoon (15mL) vodka.

4. Stir in white food coloring followed by the brown. Add more brown food coloring a drop at a time if needed.

If using molds:
5a. Slowly pour mixture into prepared lollipop molds.

If not using molds:
5b. Let the mixture cool for about 2 minutes then, using a spoon, slowly pour onto the silicone mat. Insert the lollipop sticks, being careful not to touch the hot candy. Sprinkle a generous amount of crushed peppermint onto each lollipop.

6. Let cool completely until lollipops harden and are no longer hot (about 15 minutes). Remove the lollipops from the molds or the silicone mat and wrap in lollipop bags with twist ties.

CARAMEL CHAI TEA-TINI

Caramel and chai tea are two of my favorite things, so I couldn't resist combining them for this recipe. These flavorful lollipops are indulgent without all the calories that come from milk caramels.

Makes 8–15 lollipops • Prep Time: 15 minutes • Cook Time: 15 minutes • Cooling Time: 15 minutes

1 bag chai tea

¼ cup (60mL) + 1 tablespoon (15mL) caramel flavored vodka, divided

Vegetable oil cooking spray (if using molds)

Allspice (optional)

Lollipop sticks

2 tablespoons (30mL) water

¾ cup (150g) granulated sugar

3 tablespoons (345g) corn syrup

2 drops white icing color

2 drops yellow food coloring

1 drop brown food coloring

Lollipop bags

Twist ties

1. In a small bowl, steep tea bag in ¼ cup (60mL) caramel vodka for 5 minutes. Discard the tea bag.

If using molds:
2a. Lightly coat lollipop molds with cooking spray. Sprinkle a bit of allspice in each mold (optional). Position the lollipop sticks in the grooves of the molds.

If not using molds:
2b. Place a silicone mat on a baking sheet. Position the lollipop sticks on the mat about 3 inches (76.2mm) apart so there is enough room between each.

3. Combine ¼ cup (60mL) tea-infused vodka, water, sugar, and corn syrup in a 1- or 2-quart saucepan. Place pan over medium heat to dissolve sugar. Use a wet pastry brush to "wash down" any sugar crystals that form on the side of the pan. Continue to cook the mixture without stirring until a candy thermometer registers 300 degrees.

4. Remove the pan from heat and carefully stir in the remaining tablespoon (15mL) of vodka, white icing color, yellow food coloring, and brown food coloring until completely combined. The mixture should resemble the color of caramel. Adjust as needed.

If using molds:
5a. Slowly pour mixture into prepared lollipop molds.

If not using molds:
5b. Let the mixture cool for about 2 minutes then, using a spoon, slowly pour onto the silicone mat. Adjust the lollipop sticks as needed, being careful not to touch the hot candy (the sticks should be inserted about halfway into the lollipop). Sprinkle each lollipop with a bit of allspice (optional).

6. Let cool completely until lollipops harden and are no longer hot (about 15 minutes). Remove the lollipops from the molds or the silicone mat and wrap in lollipop bags with twist ties.

STRAWBERRY-LIME CRACKED-PEPPER SMASH

Strawberries and pepper are a surprisingly tasty combination. Foodies will love this unique treat. The recipe calls for white peppercorns to infuse the vodka because black peppercorns will turn both the vodka and candy brown.

Makes 8–15 lollipops • Prep Time: 10 minutes • Cook Time: 25 minutes • Cooling Time: 15 minutes

Vegetable oil cooking spray (if using molds)

Lollipop sticks

Handful sliced dehydrated strawberries

1 cup (60mL) + 1 tablespoon (15mL) vodka, divided

1 tablespoon (6.5g) whole white peppercorns

2 tablespoons (30mL) water

¾ cup (150g) granulated sugar

3 tablespoons (245g) light corn syrup

½ teaspoon (2.5mL) natural strawberry candy oil

½ teaspoon (2.5mL) natural lime candy oil

1½ teaspoons (3g) coarsely ground black pepper

Lollipop bags

Twist ties

If using molds:
1a. Lightly coat lollipop molds with cooking spray and place 1–2 dehydrated strawberry slices and a bit of coarsely ground black pepper in the cavities of each mold. Position the lollipop sticks in the grooves of the molds.

If not using molds:
1b. Place a silicone mat on a baking sheet. Position the lollipop sticks on the mat about 3 inches (76.2mm) apart so there is enough room between each lollipop. Place 1–2 dehydrated strawberry slices above each stick.

2. Combine 1 cup vodka with peppercorns in a 1- or 2-quart saucepan. Place pan over high heat and reduce to ¼ cup (about 10 minutes). Strain the vodka through a fine mesh sieve and discard the peppercorns.

3. Combine ¼ cup (60mL) pepper-infused vodka, water, sugar, and corn syrup in a 1- or 2-quart saucepan. Place pan over medium heat to dissolve sugar. Use a wet pastry brush to "wash down" any sugar crystals that form on the side of the pan. Continue to cook the mixture without stirring until a candy thermometer registers 300 degrees.

4. Remove the pan from heat and carefully stir in remaining tablespoon vodka and candy oils.

If using molds:
5a. Slowly pour mixture into prepared lollipop molds.

If not using molds:
5b. Let the mixture cool for about 2 minutes then, using a spoon, slowly pour over the dehydrated strawberry slices. Insert the lollipop sticks, being careful not to touch the hot candy. Sprinkle each lollipop with the black pepper.

6. Let cool completely until lollipops harden and are no longer hot (about 15 minutes). Remove the lollipops from the molds or the silicone mat and wrap in lollipop bags with twist ties.

SALTED MARGARITA

What can be more fun than margaritas in lollipop form? These lollipops are a perfect addition to Cinco de Mayo and other fiesta-themed events. Package them with colorful ribbons and display in margarita glasses or mini piñatas. To spice things up even more, here are two delicious variations for a salted jalapeño margarita, add a couple drops of jalapeño candy oil at step 4. For a fruity margarita, add ¼ teaspoon of fruit-flavored candy oil.

Makes 8–15 lollipops • Prep Time: 15 minutes • Cook Time: 15 minutes • Cooling Time: 15 minutes

Vegetable oil cooking spray (if using molds)

Lollipop sticks

1 teaspoon (.9g) lime zest

½ teaspoon orange zest

¼ cup (60mL) tequila

2 tablespoons (30ml) water

¾ cup (150g) granulated sugar

3 tablespoons (245g) light corn syrup

1 drop yellow food coloring

1 teaspoon (5 mL) margarita mix

Coarse sea salt

Lollipop bags

Twist ties

If using molds:
1a. Lightly coat lollipop molds with cooking spray and place a bit of lime and orange zest in the cavities of each mold. Position the lollipop sticks in the grooves of the molds.

If not using molds:
1b. Place a silicone mat on a baking sheet. Position the lollipop sticks on the mat about 3 inches (76.2mm) apart so there is enough room between each lollipop. Place a bit of lime and orange zest above each stick.

2. Combine tequila, water, sugar, and corn syrup in a 1- or 2-quart saucepan. Place pan over medium heat to dissolve sugar. Use a wet pastry brush to "wash down" any sugar crystals that form on the side of the pan. Continue to cook the mixture without stirring until a candy thermometer registers 300 degrees.

3. Remove the pot from heat and carefully stir in food coloring and margarita mix.

If using molds:
4a. Slowly pour mixture into prepared lollipop molds. Sprinkle each lollipop with the salt.

If not using molds:
4b. Let the mixture cool for about 2 minutes then, using a spoon, slowly pour over the orange and lime zest. Adjust the lollipop sticks as needed, being careful not to touch the hot candy (the sticks should be inserted about halfway into the lollipop). Sprinkle each lollipop with the salt.

5. Let cool completely until lollipops harden and are no longer hot (about 15 minutes). Remove the lollipops from the molds or the silicone mat and wrap in lollipop bags with twist ties.

WATERMELON JALAPEÑO LIME COOLER

If you like spicy, this lollipop is for you! The flavors of watermelon, lime, and tequila are paired with fiery jalapeño for a kick. These lollipops are perfect for backyard summer barbeques and fiestas. Black sprinkles are a cute way to mimic the appearance of watermelon seeds. To make these two-tone layered lollipops, you'll need to use molds and make two batches of candy.

Makes 16 lollipops • Prep Time: 20 minutes • Cook Time: 30 minutes • Cooling Time: 30 minutes

FIRST BATCH

Vegetable oil cooking spray

Lollipop sticks

Black sprinkles (optional)

¼ cup (60mL) + 1 tablespoon (15mL) tequila, divided

2 tablespoons (30mL) water

¾ cup (150g) granulated sugar

3 tablespoons (245g) light corn syrup

2 drops red food coloring

¼ teaspoon (1.25mL) watermelon candy oil

⅛ teaspoon lime candy oil

1 drop jalapeño candy oil (getsuckered.com)

SECOND BATCH

¼ cup (60mL) + 1 tablespoon (15mL) tequila, divided

2 tablespoons (30mL) water

¾ cup (150g) granulated sugar

3 tablespoons (245g) light corn syrup

2–3 drops neon green food coloring

1 drop white icing color

¼ teaspoon (1.25mL) watermelon candy oil

⅛ teaspoon lime candy oil

1 drop jalapeño candy oil (getsuckered.com)

Lollipop bags

Twist ties

1. Lightly coat lollipop molds with cooking spray. Sprinkle black sprinkles, if using, into the cavities of each mold. Position the lollipop sticks in the grooves of the molds.

2. Combine ¼ cup (60mL) tequila, water, sugar, and corn syrup in a 1- or 2-quart saucepan. Place pan over medium heat to dissolve sugar. Use a wet pastry brush to "wash down" any sugar crystals that form on the side of the pan. Continue to cook the mixture without stirring until a candy thermometer registers 300 degrees.

3. Remove the pan from heat and carefully stir in the remaining tablespoon (15mL) of tequila, food coloring, and flavoring oils.

4. Slowly pour mixture into prepared lollipop molds filling molds up only halfway. Sprinkle black sprinkles into the red candy mixture. (optional)

5. While the first batch is cooling, repeat steps 2–3 using the ingredients listed for second batch.

6. Slowly pour mixture over the red candy, filling the molds up completely.

7. Let cool completely until lollipops harden and are no longer hot (about 15 minutes). Remove the lollipops from the molds and wrap in lollipop bags with twist ties.

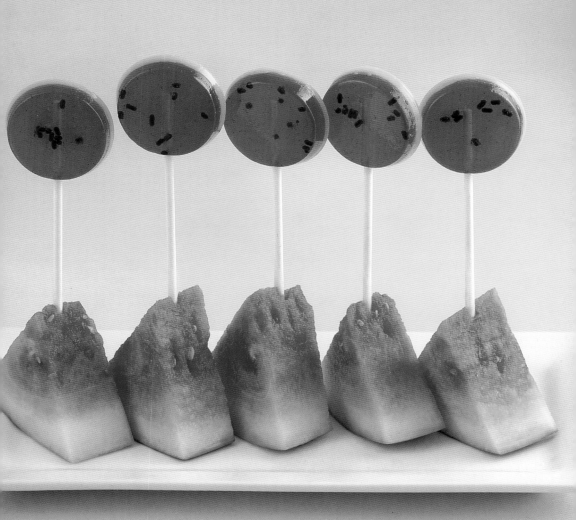

LAVENDER PALOMA

The Paloma is a traditional Mexican drink that includes tequila, grapefruit, and soda. Lavender pairs well with refreshing grapefruit and makes for a unique twist on the classic drink. This elegant lollipop would make a great addition to springtime bridal showers, weddings, and garden parties.

Makes 8–15 lollipops • Prep Time: 10 minutes • Cook Time: 15 minutes • Cooling Time: 15 minutes

Vegetable oil cooking spray (if using molds)

Lollipop sticks

3 teaspoons organic lavender buds

¼ cup (60mL) + 1 tablespoon (15mL) tequila, divided

2 tablespoons (30mL) water

¾ cup (150g) granulated sugar

3 tablespoons (245g) light corn syrup

1 drop peach or orange food coloring

1 drop food grade lavender essential oil

¼ teaspoon (1.25mL) LorAnn's natural grapefruit oil

Lollipop bags

Twist ties

If using molds:
1a. Lightly coat lollipop molds with cooking spray. Sprinkle a few lavender buds in the cavities of each mold. Position the lollipop sticks in the grooves of the molds.

If not using molds:
1b. Place a silicone mat on a baking sheet. Position the lollipop sticks on the mat about 3 inches (76.2mm) apart so there is enough room between each lollipop. Sprinkle a few lavender buds above each stick.

2. Combine ¼ cup (60mL) tequila, water, sugar, and corn syrup in a 1- or 2-quart saucepan. Place pan over medium heat to dissolve sugar. Use a wet pastry brush to "wash down" any sugar crystals that form on the side of the pan. Continue to cook the mixture without stirring until a candy thermometer registers 300 degrees.

3. Remove pan from heat and carefully stir in remaining tablespoon tequila, food coloring, and flavoring oils.

If using molds:
4a. Slowly pour mixture into prepared lollipop molds.

If not using molds:
4b. Let the mixture cool for about 2 minutes then, using a spoon, slowly pour over the lavender buds on the silicone mat. Adjust the lollipop sticks as needed, being careful not to touch the hot candy (the sticks should be inserted about halfway into the lollipop).

5. Let cool completely until lollipops harden and are no longer hot (about 15 minutes). Remove the lollipops from the molds or the silicone mat and wrap in lollipop bags with twist ties.

MINT JULEP

These are an absolute must for Kentucky Derby and Southern-themed parties. Arrange them in the pewter cups that mint juleps are traditionally served in for a fun display.

Makes 8–15 lollipops • Prep Time: 10 minutes • Cook Time: 15 minutes • Cooling Time: 15 minutes

Vegetable oil cooking spray (if using molds)

Lollipop sticks

1 small bunch fresh mint leaves

¼ cup (60mL) + 1 tablespoon (15mL) bourbon, divided

2 tablespoons (60mL) water

¾ cup (150g) granulated sugar

3 tablespoons (245g) light corn syrup

1 drop brown food coloring (optional)

Lollipop bags

Twist ties

If using molds:
1a. Lightly coat lollipop molds with cooking spray and place 1–2 mint leaves in the cavities of each mold. Position the lollipop sticks in the grooves of the molds.

If not using molds:
1b. Place a silicone mat on a baking sheet. Position the lollipop sticks on the mat about 3 inches (76.3mm) apart so there is enough room between each lollipop. Place 1–2 mint leaves above each stick where you intend to pour the candy syrup.

2. Combine ¼ cup (60mL) bourbon, water, sugar, and corn syrup in a 1- or 2-quart saucepan. Place pan over medium heat to dissolve sugar. Use a wet pastry brush to "wash down" any sugar crystals that form on the side of the pan. Continue to cook the mixture without stirring until a candy thermometer registers 300 degrees.

3. Remove the pot from heat and carefully stir in food coloring (optional) and remaining tablespoon of bourbon.

If using molds:
4a. Slowly pour mixture into prepared lollipop molds.

If not using molds:
4b. Let the mixture cool for about 2 minutes then, using a spoon, slowly pour over the mint leaves. Adjust the lollipop sticks as needed, being careful not to touch the hot candy (the sticks should be inserted about halfway into the lollipop).

5. Let cool completely until lollipops harden and are no longer hot (about 15 minutes). Remove the lollipops from the molds or the silicone mat and wrap in lollipop bags with twist ties.

BLACKBERRY SAGE JULEP

I absolutely love using herbs in cocktails. This lollipop is inspired by one of my favorite herbal drinks. Sage can easily overpower a recipe so don't be tempted to use more than a few small pieces in each lollipop. The rich color of these lollipops is incredibly pretty when paired with edible gold dust. Simply brush a bit of the dust onto the lollipops after they harden.

Makes 8–15 lollipops • Prep Time: 15 minutes • Cook Time: 15 minutes • Cooling Time: 15 minutes

Vegetable oil cooking spray (if using molds)

Lollipop sticks

1–2 fresh sage leaves, chopped

1 teaspoon (5mL) of edible gold dust (optional)

15-20 dehydrated blackberries (optional)

¼ cup (60mL) + 1 tablespoon (15mL) bourbon, divided

2 tablespoons (30mL) water

¾ cup (150g) granulated sugar

3 tablespoons (245g) light corn syrup

1 drop burgundy food coloring (or a drop red food coloring and a drop purple food coloring)

¼ teaspoon (1.25mL) blackberry candy oil

Lollipop bags

Twist ties

If using molds:
1a. Lightly coat lollipop molds with cooking spray and place a few pieces of dehydrated blackberry (if using) and chopped sage leaf in the cavities of each mold. Position the lollipop sticks in the grooves of the molds.

If not using molds:
1b. Place a silicone mat on a baking sheet. Position the lollipop sticks on the mat about 3 inches (76.2mm) apart so there is enough room between each lollipop. Place a few pieces of dehydrated blackberry (if using) and chopped sage leaf above each stick where you intend to pour the candy syrup.

2. Combine ¼ cup (60mL) bourbon, water, sugar, and corn syrup in a 1- or 2-quart saucepan. Place pan over medium heat to dissolve sugar. Use a wet pastry brush to "wash down" any sugar crystals that form on the side of the pan. Continue to cook the mixture without stirring until a candy thermometer registers 300 degrees.

3. Remove the pan from heat and carefully stir in remaining tablespoon bourbon, food coloring, and candy oil.

If using molds:
4a. Slowly pour mixture into prepared lollipop molds.

If not using molds:
4b. Let the mixture cool for about 2 minutes then, using a spoon, slowly pour over the dehydrated blackberries (if using) and sage leaves. Adjust the lollipop sticks as needed, being careful not to touch the hot candy (the sticks should be inserted about halfway into the lollipop).

5. Let cool completely until lollipops harden and are no longer hot (about 15 minutes). Remove the lollipops from the molds or the silicone mat and wrap in lollipop bags with twist ties.

CINNAMON KISS

These subtly flavored cinnamon lollipops make for a flirtatious Valentine's gift or party favor. Use lip or heart-shaped molds to fit the theme. A generous sprinkling of edible glitter adds a lot of va-va-voom.

Makes 8–15 lollipops • Prep Time: 15 minutes • Cook Time: 15 minutes • Cooling Time: 15 minutes

Vegetable oil cooking spray (if using molds)

Lollipop sticks

1 teaspoon (5mL) of red edible glitter (optional)

¼ cup (60mL) + 1 tablespoon (15mL) cinnamon whiskey, divided

2 tablespoons (30mL) water

¾ cup (150g) granulated sugar

3 tablespoons (245g) light corn syrup

2-3 drops red food coloring

Lollipop bags

Twist ties

If using molds:
1a. Lightly coat lollipop molds with cooking spray and sprinkle edible glitter (if using) in the cavities of each mold. Position the lollipop sticks in the grooves of the molds.

If not using molds:
1b. Place a silicone mat on a baking sheet. Position the lollipop sticks on the mat about 3 inches (76.2mm) apart so there is enough room between each lollipop.

2. Combine ¼ cup (60mL) whiskey, water, sugar, and corn syrup in a 1- or 2-quart saucepan. Place pan over medium heat to dissolve sugar. Use a wet pastry brush to "wash down" any sugar crystals that form on the side of the pan. Continue to cook the mixture without stirring until a candy thermometer registers 300 degrees.

3. Remove the pan from heat and carefully stir in remaining tablespoon whiskey and food coloring.

If using molds:
4a. Slowly pour mixture into prepared lollipop molds.

If not using molds:
4b. Let the mixture cool for about 2 minutes then, using a spoon, slowly pour over the lollipop sticks on the silicone mat. Adjust the lollipop sticks as needed, being careful not to touch the hot candy (the sticks should be inserted about halfway into the lollipop). Sprinkle a bit of edible glitter (if using) on each lollipop.

5. Let cool completely until lollipops harden and are no longer hot (about 15 minutes). Remove the lollipops from the molds or the silicone mat and wrap in lollipop bags with twist ties.

VANILLA BEAN OLD-FASHIONED

I get so excited about anything made with vanilla bean. Vanilla bean can be used in so much more than sweets and desserts—it's also a great addition to cocktails, especially those made with whiskey.

Makes 8–15 lollipops • Prep Time: 15 minutes • Cook Time: 15 minutes • Cooling Time: 15 minutes

Vegetable oil cooking spray (if using molds)

Lollipop sticks

Thin slices orange peel (one slice per lollipop)

¼ cup (60mL) + 1 teaspoon (15mL) bourbon, divided

2 tablespoons (30mL) water

¾ cup (150g) granulated sugar

3 tablespoons (245g) light corn syrup

½ teaspoon (2.5mL) orange bitters (optional)

1 teaspoon (16g) vanilla bean paste

Lollipop bags

Twist ties

If using molds:
1a. Lightly coat lollipop molds with cooking spray and place 1 orange peel in the cavity of each mold. Position the lollipop sticks in the grooves of the molds.

If not using molds:
1b. Place a silicone mat on a baking sheet. Position the lollipop sticks on the mat about 3 inches (76.2mm) apart so there is enough room between each lollipop. Place 1 orange peel above each stick where you intend to pour the candy syrup.

2. Combine ¼ cup (60mL) bourbon, water, sugar, and corn syrup in a 1- or 2-quart saucepan. Place pan over medium heat to dissolve sugar. Use a wet pastry brush to "wash down" any sugar crystals that form on the side of the pan. Continue to cook the mixture without stirring until a candy thermometer registers 300 degrees. Remove the pot from heat and carefully stir in the remaining teaspoon bourbon, vanilla bean paste, and bitters (optional).

If using molds:
3a. Slowly pour mixture into prepared lollipop molds.

If not using molds:
3b. Let the mixture cool for about 2 minutes then, using a spoon, slowly pour over the orange peel and lollipop sticks. Adjust the lollipop sticks as needed, being careful not to touch the hot candy (the sticks should be inserted about halfway into the lollipop).

4. Let cool completely until lollipops harden and are no longer hot (about 15 minutes). Remove the lollipops from the molds or the silicone mat and wrap in lollipop bags with twist ties.

SPIKED EGGNOG

The holidays simply aren't complete without eggnog. These lollipops make great hostess gifts, stocking stuffers, and gift toppers. If you use plastic lollipop sticks, they can also double as beverage stirrers to impart flavor to coffee or hot chocolate.

Makes 8–15 lollipops • Prep Time: 15 minutes • Cook Time: 15 minutes • Cooling Time: 15 minutes

Vegetable oil cooking spray (if using molds)

Lollipop sticks

Pinch or two ground nutmeg

¼ cup (60mL) + 1 tablespoon (15mL) bourbon, divided

2 tablespoons (30mL) water

¾ cup (150g) granulated sugar

3 tablespoons (245g) light corn syrup

2–3 drops white icing color

⅛ teaspoon eggnog-flavored candy oil

Lollipop bags

Twist ties

If using molds:

1a. Lightly coat lollipop molds with cooking spray and sprinkle a bit of nutmeg in the cavities of each mold. Position the lollipop sticks in the grooves of the molds.

If not using molds:

1b. Place a silicone mat on a baking sheet. Position the lollipop sticks on the mat about 3 inches (76.2mm) apart so there is enough room between each lollipop. (The nutmeg will be sprinkled after the lollipops have been poured.)

2. Combine ¼ cup (60mL) bourbon, water, sugar, and corn syrup in a 1- or 2-quart saucepan. Place pan over medium heat to dissolve sugar. Use a wet pastry brush to "wash down" any sugar crystals that form on the side of the pan. Continue to cook the mixture without stirring until a candy thermometer registers 300 degrees.

3. Remove the pan from heat and carefully stir in the remaining tablespoon bourbon, white icing color, and eggnog candy oil.

If using molds:

4a. Slowly pour mixture into prepared lollipop molds.

If not using molds:

4b. Let the mixture cool for about 2 minutes then, using a spoon, slowly pour over the lollipop sticks on the silicone mat. Adjust the lollipop sticks as needed, being careful not to touch the hot candy (the sticks should be inserted about halfway into the lollipop). Sprinkle each lollipop with a bit of nutmeg.

5. Let cool completely until lollipops harden and are no longer hot (about 15 minutes). Remove the lollipops from the molds or the silicone mat and wrap in lollipop bags with twist ties.

RASPBERRY ROSE GIN RICKEY

I first learned about the Rickey cocktail when I was going to school back east (it was created in Washington, D.C., in the nineteenth century). A basic Rickey consists of gin or bourbon, lime juice, and carbonated water. It's like the American version of a mojito. I spruced up the basic recipe with raspberry, rose flavoring, and rose petals for these pretty lollipops.

Makes 8–15 lollipops • Prep Time: 10 minutes • Cook Time: 15 minutes • Cooling Time: 15 minutes

Vegetable oil cooking spray (if using molds)

Lollipop sticks

Handful organic dried rose petals (optional)

½ teaspoon (.9g) of lime zest

¼ cup (60mL) + 1 tablespoon (15mL) gin, divided

2 tablespoons (30mL) water

¾ cup (150g) granulated sugar

3 tablespoons (245g) light corn syrup

⅛ teaspoon rose flavored candy oil

⅛ teaspoon raspberry candy oil

¼ teaspoon (1.25mL) lime candy oil

2 drops lime food coloring (optional)

Lollipop bags

Twist ties

If using molds:

1a. Lightly coat lollipop molds with cooking spray and sprinkle lime zest and a few rose petals (if using) in the cavities of each mold. Position the lollipop sticks in the grooves of the molds.

If not using molds:

1b. Place a silicone mat on a baking sheet. Position the lollipop sticks on the mat about 3 inches (76.2mm) apart so there is enough room between each lollipop. Sprinkle lime zest and a few rose petals (if using) above each stick where you intend to pour the candy.

2. Combine ¼ cup (60mL) gin, water, sugar, and corn syrup in a 1- or 2-quart saucepan. Place pan over medium heat to dissolve sugar. Use a wet pastry brush to "wash down" any sugar crystals that form on the side of the pan. Continue to cook the mixture without stirring until a candy thermometer registers 300 degrees.

3. Remove pan from heat and carefully stir in remaining tablespoon (15mL) gin, food coloring (if using), and candy oils.

If using molds:

4a. Slowly pour mixture into prepared lollipop molds.

If not using molds:

4b. Let the mixture cool for about 2 minutes then, using a spoon, slowly pour onto the silicone mat over the lime zest and rose petals. Adjust the lollipop sticks as needed, being careful not to touch the hot candy (the sticks should be inserted about halfway into the lollipop).

5. Let cool completely until lollipops harden and are no longer hot (about 15 minutes). Remove the lollipops from the molds or the silicone mat and wrap in lollipop bags with twist ties.

ROSEMARY SALTY DOG LOLLIPOP

These lollipops are based on another one of my favorite cocktails, the Salty Dog. Refreshing grapefruit paired with fragrant rosemary makes for a great flavor. Finishing the lollipops off with sea salt adds complexity.

Makes 8–15 lollipops • Prep Time: 15 minutes • Cook Time: 15 minutes • Cooling Time: 15 minutes

Vegetable oil cooking spray (if using molds)

Lollipop sticks

10–12 leaves of rosemary

½ teaspoon (.9g) grapefruit zest

¼ cup (60mL) + 1 tablespoon (5mL) gin, divided

2 tablespoons (30mL) water

¾ cup (150g) granulated sugar

3 tablespoons (245g) corn syrup

¼ teaspoon (1.25mL) LorAnn's natural grapefruit oil

1 drop pink or orange food coloring (optional)

1 tablespoon (15mL) of course sea salt

Lollipop bags

Twist ties

If using molds:

1a. Lightly coat lollipop molds with cooking spray and sprinkle a bit of grapefruit zest and 2–3 rosemary leaves in the cavities of each mold. Position the lollipop sticks in the grooves of the molds.

If not using molds:

1b. Place a silicone mat on a baking sheet. Position the lollipop sticks on the mat about 3 inches (76.2mm) apart so there is enough room between each lollipop. Sprinkle a bit of grapefruit zest and 2–3 rosemary leaves above each stick where you intend to pour the candy.

2. Combine ¼ cup (60mL) gin, water, sugar, and corn syrup in a 1- or 2-quart saucepan. Place pan over medium heat to dissolve sugar. Use a wet pastry brush to "wash down" any sugar crystals that form on the side of the pan. Continue to cook the mixture without stirring until a candy thermometer registers 300 degrees.

3. Remove the pan from heat and carefully stir in remaining tablespoon (15mL) gin, essential oil, and food coloring (if using).

If using molds:

4a. Slowly pour mixture into prepared lollipop molds. Sprinkle each lollipop with a pinch sea salt.

If not using molds:

4b. Let the mixture cool for about 2 minutes then, using a spoon, slowly pour onto the silicone mat over the zest and rosemary. Adjust the lollipop sticks as needed, being careful not to touch the hot candy (the sticks should be inserted about halfway into the lollipop). Sprinkle each lollipop with pinch sea salt.

5. Let cool completely until lollipops harden and are no longer hot (about 15 minutes). Remove the lollipops from the molds or the silicone mat and wrap in lollipop bags with twist ties.

CUCUMBER BASIL GIMLET

Cucumber is another one of my favorite cocktail additions. Because cucumbers are so hydrating, I've convinced myself that I'm essentially canceling out the dehydrating effect liquor has on the body. Whether that's true or not, with these lollipops you can avoid the hangover while still enjoying the refreshing taste of cucumber paired with basil, lime, and gin.

Makes 8–15 lollipops • Prep Time: 15 minutes • Cook Time: 15 minutes • Cooling Time: 15 minutes

Vegetable oil cooking spray (if using molds)

Lollipop sticks

½ teaspoon (.9g) lime zest

3–5 large basil leaves, chopped

¼ cup (60mL) + 1 teaspoon (5mL) gin, divided

2 tablespoons (30mL) water

¾ cup (150g) granulated sugar

3 tablespoons (245g) corn syrup

¼ teaspoon (1.25mL) cucumber candy oil (perfumersapprentice.com)

⅛ teaspoon lime candy oil

If using molds:
1a. Lightly coat lollipop molds with cooking spray and sprinkle a bit of lime zest and basil leaves in the cavities of each mold. Position the lollipop sticks in the grooves of the molds.

If not using molds:
1b. Place a silicone mat on a baking sheet. Position the lollipop sticks on the mat about 3 inches (76.2mm) apart so there is enough room between each lollipop. Sprinkle lime zest and basil leaves above each stick where you intend to pour the candy.

2. Combine ¼ cup (60mL) gin, water, sugar, and corn syrup in a 1- or 2-quart saucepan. Place pan over medium heat to dissolve sugar. Use a wet pastry brush to "wash down" any sugar crystals that form on the side of the pan. Continue to cook the mixture without stirring until a candy thermometer registers 300 degrees.

3. Remove the pot from heat and carefully stir in remaining tablespoon (15mL) gin and candy oils.

If using molds:
4a. Slowly pour mixture into prepared lollipop molds.

If not using molds:
4b. Let the mixture cool for about 2 minutes then, using a spoon, slowly pour onto the silicone mat over the lime zest and basil. Adjust the lollipop sticks as needed, being careful not to touch the hot candy (the sticks should be inserted about halfway into the lollipop).

5. Let cool completely until lollipops harden and are no longer hot (about 15 minutes). Remove the lollipops from the molds or the silicone mat and wrap in lollipop bags with twist ties.

LIQUOR
CANDY

ACCESSORIES

CHAMPAGNE STIRRERS

These cocktail stirrers are a fun and elegant twist on the Kir Royale, a cocktail made with champagne and black currant liqueur. The champagne takes on the flavor of the lollipop as it is stirred. The addition of edible gold leaf is an especially nice touch for New Year's Eve. Replace the black currant flavoring with peach flavoring to make a Kir Peche or with raspberry flavoring to make a Kir Framboise. Use wooden skewers or plastic lollipop sticks instead of paper lollipop sticks because regular paper lollipop sticks will unravel in the drink..

Makes 30 lollipops • Prep Time: 10 minutes • Cook Time: 15 minutes • Cooling Time: 15 minutes

Vegetable oil cooking spray

30 wooden skewers trimmed to the length of the champagne glass

½ cup (120mL) water

1 cup (200g) granulated sugar

⅓ cup (108g) light corn syrup

1 drop burgundy food coloring (or a drop red and a drop purple food coloring)

¼ teaspoon (1.25mL) black currant candy oil

Edible gold leaf flakes or edible gold sprinkles (optional)

Lollipop bags

Twist ties

Note: Stir the lollipops in the champagne. As they dissolve it will infuse your glass with a delicious sweet flavor.

1. Lightly coat 1.5-inch (38mm) round lollipop molds with cooking spray.

2. Position wooden skewers in the grooves of the molds.

3. Combine water, sugar, and corn syrup in a 1- or 2-quart saucepan. Place pan over medium heat to dissolve sugar. Use a wet pastry brush to "wash down" any sugar crystals that form on the side of the pan. Continue to cook the mixture without stirring until a candy thermometer registers 300 degrees.

4. Remove the pan from heat and carefully stir in food coloring, black currant candy oil, and a generous amount of gold leaf flakes (if using).

5. Slowly pour mixture into prepared lollipop molds.

6. Let cool completely until lollipops harden and are no longer hot (about 15 minutes). Remove the lollipops from the molds. Serve in a glass of champagne.

VALENTINE'S SHOT GLASSES

These beautiful red candy shot glasses are sure to make your Valentine's Day special. Keep in mind, the liquor of your choice once placed inside the glasses will take on the flavor of the candy.

Makes 4 shot glasses • Prep Time: 5 minutes • Cook Time: 15 minutes • Cooling Time: 25 minutes

¾ cup (180mL) water

2 cups (400g) granulated sugar

⅔ cup (160mL) light corn syrup

½ cup (120mL) of honey, agave, or simple syrup

3 teaspoons (15mL) of heart shaped sprinkles

3 teaspoons (15mL) of red or pink edible glitter

½ cup (120mL) of red or pink colored sugar

1. Combine the water, sugar, and corn syrup in a 1- or 2-quart saucepan. Place pan over medium heat to dissolve sugar. Use wet pastry brush to "wash down" any sugar crystals that form on the side of the pan. Continue to cook the mixture without stirring until a candy thermometer registers 300 degrees.

2. Remove the pot from heat and carefully stir in heart shaped sprinkles and pink or red edible glitter in to the candy mixture.

3. Slowly pour the mixture into the shot glass mold.

4. Let cool completely until the candy hardens and is no longer hot (about 25 minutes). Remove the glasses from the molds. Dip the rims of the glasses into a small bowl of either honey, agave, or simple syrup. Then, dip the glasses into a small bowl of red or pink colored sugar to decorate the rim.

LUXE GOLD SHOT GLASSES

These elegant golden beauties are a wonderful addition to bridal receptions or anniversary parties. Keep in mind, the liquor of your choice once placed inside the glasses will take on the flavor of the candy.

Makes 4 shot glasses • Prep Time: 5 minutes • Cook Time: 15 minutes • Cooling Time: 25 minutes

¾ cup (180mL) water

2 cups (400g) granulated sugar

⅔ cup (160mL) light corn syrup

½ cup (120mL) of honey, agave, or simple syrup

3 teaspoons (15mL) of edible gold leaf flakes

½ cup (120mL) of gold colored sugar (optional)

1. Combine the water, sugar, and corn syrup in a 1- or 2-quart saucepan. Place pan over medium heat to dissolve sugar. Use wet pastry brush to "wash down" any sugar crystals that form on the side of the pan. Continue to cook the mixture without stirring until a candy thermometer registers 300 degrees.

2. Remove the pot from heat and carefully stir in edible gold leaf flakes. Slowly pour the mixture into the shot glass mold.

3. Let cool completely until the candy hardens and is no longer hot (about 25 minutes). Remove the glasses from the molds. Dip the rims of the glasses into a small bowl of either honey, agave, or simple syrup. Then, dip the glasses into a small bowl of gold colored sugar to decorate the rim.

Birthday Cake Shot Glasses

These hard candy shot glasses will be the talk of the party! They are easy to make and fun and unique way to celebrate someone's special day. Keep in mind, the liquor of your choice once placed inside the glasses will take on the flavor of the candy.

Makes 4 shot glasses • Prep Time: 5 minutes • Cook Time: 15 minutes • Cooling Time: 25 minutes

¾ cup (180mL) water

2 cups (400g) granulated sugar

⅔ cup (160mL) light corn syrup

½ cup (120mL) of honey, agave, or simple syrup

2–3 drops of white food coloring

2–3 drops of yellow food coloring

¼ teaspoon (1.25mL) cake flavored candy oil

1 cup (240mL) of rainbow sprinkles

1. Combine the water, sugar, and corn syrup in a 1- or 2-quart saucepan. Place pan over medium heat to dissolve sugar. Use wet pastry brush to "wash down" any sugar crystals that form on the side of the pan. Continue to cook the mixture without stirring until a candy thermometer registers 300 degrees.

2. Remove the pot from heat and carefully stir in the rainbow sprinkles and the cake candy oil flavoring.

3. Slowly pour the mixture into the shot glass mold.

4. Let cool completely until the candy hardens and is no longer hot (about 25 minutes). Remove the glasses from the molds. Dip the rims of the glasses into a small bowl of either honey, agave, or simple syrup. Then, dip the glasses into a small bowl of rainbow sprinkles to decorate the rim.

HOLIDAY PEPPERMINT SHOT GLASSES

These holiday treats are a fun addition to any Christmas gathering. Everyone will love drinking shots from these and then snacking on them afterwards!

Makes 4 shot glasses • Prep Time: 5 minutes • Cook Time: 15 minutes • Cooling Time: 25 minutes

¾ cup (180mL) water

2 cups (400g) granulated sugar

⅔ cup (160mL) light corn syrup

½ cup (120mL) of honey, agave, or simple syrup

2–3 drops of white food coloring

2–3 drops of yellow food coloring

1/8 teaspoon (1.25mL) peppermint flavored candy oil

½ cup (120mL) of red or white colored sugar (optional)

1. Combine the water, sugar, and corn syrup in a 1- or 2-quart saucepan. Place pan over medium heat to dissolve sugar. Use wet pastry brush to "wash down" any sugar crystals that form on the side of the pan. Continue to cook the mixture without stirring until a candy thermometer registers 300 degrees.

2. Remove the pot from heat and carefully stir in white food coloring and stir. Add peppermint candy oil and stir. Add a drop of red food coloring and gently swirl in a figure 8 pattern to create a marbled effect.

Another option for this recipe is to place a row of round peppermint or spearmint candies at the bottom of the mold (this will be the lip of the shot glass). Then, add red or white food coloring and peppermint flavored oil and stir.

3. Slowly pour the mixture into the shot glass mold.

4. Let cool completely until the candy hardens and is no longer hot (about 25 minutes). Remove the glasses from the molds. Dip the rims of the glasses into a small bowl of either honey, agave, or simple syrup. Then, dip the glasses into a small bowl of red or white colored sugar to decorate the rim.

CANDY CORN SHOT GLASSES

These charming candy shot glasses are the perfect addition to all of your Halloween festivities! Keep in mind, the liquor of your choice once placed inside the glasses will take on the flavor of the candy.

Makes 4 shot glasses • Prep Time: 10 minutes • Cook Time: 30 minutes • Cooling Time: 45 minutes

FIRST BATCH

¾ cup (180mL) water

2 cups (400g) granulated sugar

⅔ cup (160mL) light corn syrup

½ cup (120mL) of honey, agave, or simple syrup

2–3 drops of white food coloring

2–3 drops of orange food coloring

2–3 drops of yellow food coloring

¼ teaspoon (1.25mL) candy corn flavored candy oil

SECOND BATCH

¾ cup (180mL) water

2 cups (400g) granulated sugar

⅔ cup (160mL) light corn syrup

2–3 drops of white food coloring

2–3 drops of yellow food coloring

¼ teaspoon (1.25mL) candy corn flavored candy oil

½ cup (120mL) of orange colored sugar

Whipped cream

1. Combine the water, sugar, and corn syrup in a 1- or 2-quart saucepan. Place pan over medium heat to dissolve sugar. Use wet pastry brush to "wash down" any sugar crystals that form on the side of the pan. Continue to cook the mixture without stirring until a candy thermometer registers 300 degrees.

2. Remove the pot from heat and carefully stir in white and yellow food coloring and stir until colors are thoroughly mixed. Add candy corn flavoring oil (available at Getsuckered.com/ Fall Candy Oil 5 Flavor Assortment) and stir.

3. Slowly pour the mixture into the shot glass mold only halfway.

4. Let the yellow portion of the shot glasses cool for 15 minutes.

5a. Make a second batch of candy. Add candy corn flavoring, white and orange food coloring and stir until colors are thoroughly mixed. Pour over the yellow portion of the shot glasses until molds are full.

5b. Let cool completely until the candy hardens and is no longer hot (about 25 minutes). Remove the glasses from the molds. Dip the rims of the glasses into a small bowl of either honey, agave, or simple syrup. Then, dip the glasses into a small bowl of orange colored sugar to decorate the rim.

6. When serving, top the shots off with whipped cream to complete the appearance of candy corn.

ABOUT THE AUTHOR

Kristina Maury is the founder of Luxe Lollies, a Los Angeles–based business that specializes in gourmet, handcrafted lollipops with an emphasis on custom creations.

Luxe Lollies was founded in 2012, but Kristina's interest in candy making goes back to her childhood when she got the idea to melt sugar in a kitchen skillet while home alone one day. Working without a recipe, she added her grandmother's raspberry coffee syrup for flavor. Looking back, the end result was a catastrophe, but 12-year-old Kristina was delighted with the amber-colored mass of burnt sugar that tasted more bitter than fruity. Considering she was completely unaware of how dangerous hot caramelized sugar can be, it's a miracle she didn't get burned, too. Though her technique and emphasis on safety have greatly improved, her zeal for experimentation remains the same.

As the years passed, Kristina lost touch with her inner confectioner and went on to receive a B.A. in journalism at Howard University and a law degree from Harvard. Oddly enough, law school reignited her creativity. She often found herself making gourmet treats like candy corn– and bubble-gum-flavored cupcakes to relieve stress. After she graduated, she dabbled in law for a bit and decided it wasn't the right career path for her. While trying to figure out what to do with her life, she turned to candy making (specifically lollipop making) again to cope and soon realized that she could sell her candy to make money in the meantime. She noticed there was a lack of high-end, gourmet hard candies in the marketplace and decided to focus on making lollipops for people with sophisticated palates. As the demand for her products grew, she decided that this was something she could pursue full-time.

Kristina has custom designed lollipops for several big companies and her products have been featured in numerous publications including *Southern Weddings* magazine. Industry magazine *Candy & Snack Today* included Luxe Lollies in a list of businesses "thriving in the customized candy" industry.

Kristina was the first to offer a virtual "Design Your Own Lollipop" experience to her customers. This web-based function allows users to design their own lollipop while watching it develop onscreen. Customers can select from thousands of flavor and ingredient combinations, a large variety of lollipop and ribbon colors, and customized label designs.

Kristina lives in Rancho Palos Verdes, California, with her Bichon Frise, Butch. She gets her inspiration from fashion and beauty trends, cocktails, desserts, and interior design. She is also inspired by the concept of taking items usually associated with childhood and making them more sophisticated.